GUY STUFF
FEELINGS

EVERYTHING you need to KNOW about YOUR EMOTIONS

BY DR. CARA NATTERSON | ILLUSTRATED BY MICAH PLAYER

Editorial Development: Barbara E. Stretchberry
Art Direction and Design: Gretchen Becker
Production: Jessica Bernard, Caryl Boyer, Cynthia Stiles, Heather Tubwon
Illustrations: Micah Player

This book is not intended to replace the advice of or treatment by health-care professionals. It should be considered an additional resource only. Questions and concerns about mental or physical health should always be discussed with a doctor or other health-care professional.

Cataloging-in-Publication data available from the Library of Congress

© 2021 American Girl. All American Girl marks are trademarks of American Girl. Marcas registradas utilizadas bajo licencia. American Girl ainsi que les marques et designs y afférents appartiennent à American Girl. **MADE IN CHINA. HECHO EN CHINA. FABRIQUÉ EN CHINE.** Retain this address for future reference: American Girl, 8400 Fairway Place, Middleton, WI 53562, U.S.A. **Importado y distribuido por** A.G. México Retail, S. de R.L. de C.V., Miguel de Cervantes Saavedra No. 193 Pisos 10 y 11, Col. Granada, Delegación Miguel Hidalgo, C.P. 11520 Ciudad de México. D.F. Conserver ces informations pour s'y référer en cas de besoin. American Girl Canada, 8400 Fairway Place, Middleton, WI 53562, U.S.A. **Manufactured for and imported into the EU by:** Mattel Europa B.V., Gondel 1, 1186 MJ Amstelveen, Nederland.

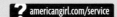 americangirl.com/service

a LETTER to YOU GUYS,

Growing up means changes in your body, but it also means that your feelings and emotions are growing and changing, too. Emotions are part of being human—crying when we're hurt, laughing when we are amused, feeling frustrated when things don't go our way, and fuming when someone does something that's really not OK. Sometimes our emotions are small, but other times they are so strong that they feel as if they might overpower our clear thinking, and occasionally they do.

When you were younger, your feelings were probably pretty easy to understand, but now that you're growing up, feelings are getting bigger and more complicated. Maybe this has already begun. And you can experience a whole bunch of emotions at one time, which can feel confusing.

Some guys don't think they need to get in touch with their feelings, while other guys try but have trouble putting words to them. Learning what you're feeling and why will help you be in better control of your life. It's an important part of growing up—and of taking charge of your mind and body. Let's do this!

YOUR FRIENDS
♡ at GUY STUFF

CONTENTS

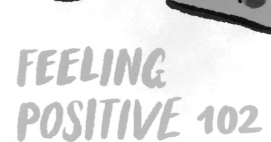

Everyone experiences feelings all day, every day. Emotions can go from happy to sad, angry to scared, calm to annoyed, frustrated to victorious. Sometimes feelings carry physical sensations along with them—such as a bellyache or a stream of tears or a racing heartbeat. Other times feelings just swirl around inside in the form of thoughts. These emotions can be big, completely shifting your mood and behavior. Or they can be so tiny that you barely notice them. They can last a long time, or they can shift in a minute. All of this can be confusing until you learn how to sort through how you feel and why.

WHAT are FEELINGS, exactly?

When something happens to us—or even just around us— we react. That reaction is called a feeling or an emotion.

Every minute of every day, people are talking, events are unfolding, the world is changing. Each person has his or her own response to what's going on at that moment. A joke can be funny to one person but hurtful to another. A stunt can be scary for this guy but super fun for that guy. When you attach a name to your reaction, it becomes easier to understand how you feel.

The way you feel might not be the same as the way someone else feels, even someone who is standing right next to you looking at or hearing the exact same thing. In the same way that no one knows what you are thinking unless they ask, you will never really know how someone else feels unless you ask them. This is why we try to put words to our emotions.

Only you know how you feel inside. Your best friends or your parents can sometimes guess what's going on based on how you look or act, but they won't know for sure unless you tell them. And you can't tell them unless you have words to describe your emotions.

I FELT...

There are lots of different emotions, and each one can be described in many ways.

Take a look at these words. Which ones are more general? Which ones describe a feeling in more detail? Which words are strong and forceful? Do some suggest that a feeling is more important while others make a feeling seem like less of a big deal?

HOW ARE YOU?

ALONE *isolated* RELUCTANT *nervous*

WARY *afraid* CAREFUL

RESERVED *embarrassed*

SHY

SHRINKING BASHFUL CAUTIOUS HESITANT Quiet *timid*

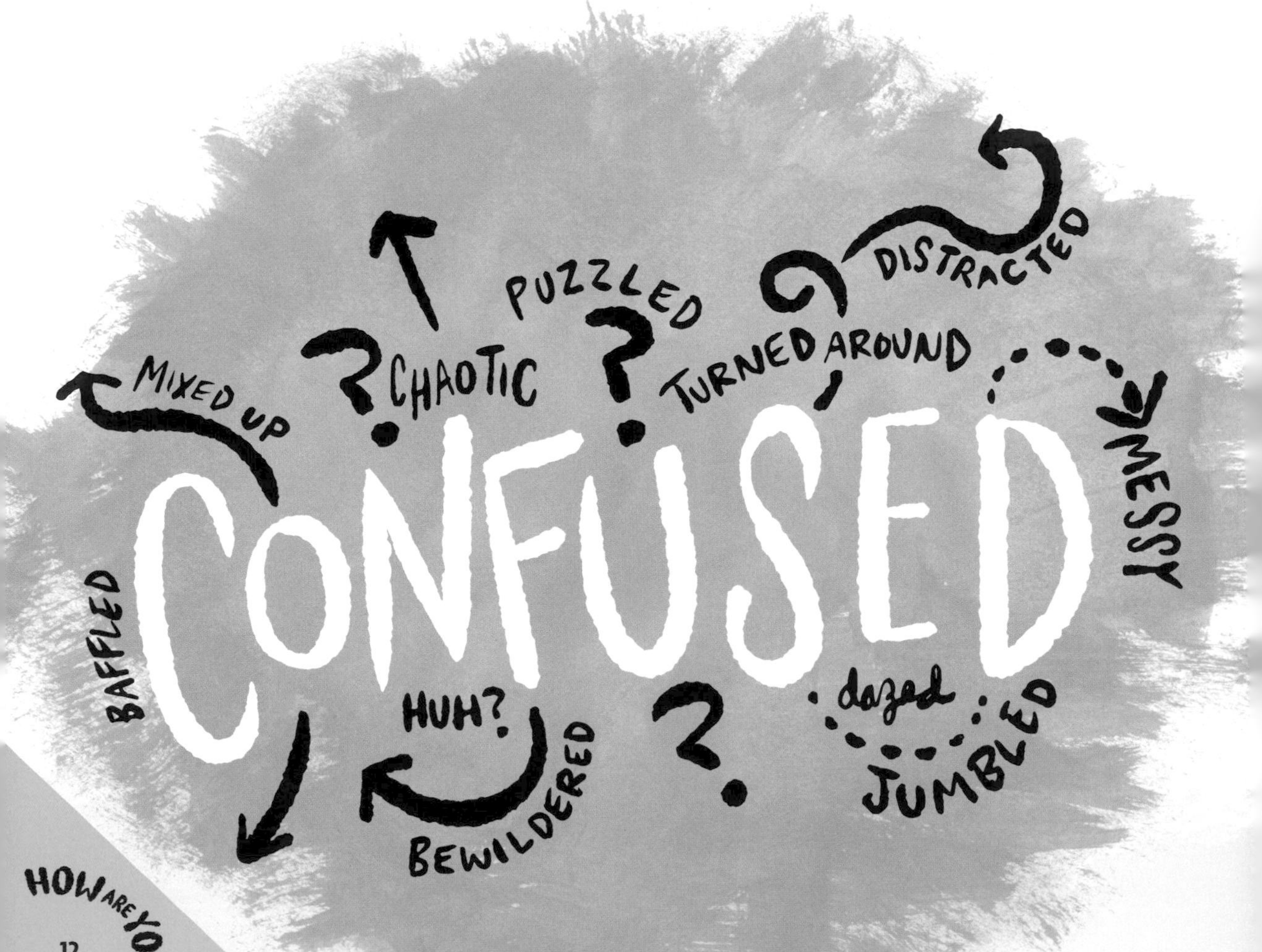

PUZZLED

DISTRACTED

MIXED UP

CHAOTIC ?

TURNED AROUND

MESSY

BAFFLED

CONFUSED

HUH?

BEWILDERED

?

dazed

JUMBLED

NERVOUS ★ EAGER ★ MOTIVATED Revved UP

DELIGHTED

WIRED

AMPED

ENERGETIC

EXCITED

FIRED UP JUMPY jazzed

HEAVY-HEARTED

SHEEPISH SAD

REGRETFUL EMBARRASSED

APOLOGETIC

UNHAPPY

sorry

CONTRITE SORROWFUL

Choosing a specific word to describe how you feel can help others understand you better. It can help you better understand yourself, too.

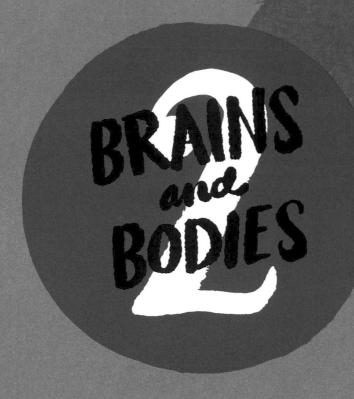

BRAINS and BODIES 2

When you see, touch, smell, or hear something, your brain receives that information and then tells your body how to react, often in an instant. Your heart might begin to race, or your stomach may suddenly feel like it is filled with butterflies. These physical sensations are created when your brain takes in what's happening and tells your body how to act in response.

BRAIN POWER

The brain turns feelings into physical movements and sensations.

The brain is a collection of millions of cells called *neurons* packed inside your head. These neurons connect with other neurons throughout your entire body, creating a network that can send messages from your head to your toes. When a bunch of neurons are bundled together, they are called *nerves*.

Let's say you touch a hot pan. Your finger burns. You will jerk your hand away from the pan, right? Yes, but only because the nerves in your fingers sent a message to your brain telling it that there is something painful coming into contact with that part of your body—then your brain zipped a message along a different set of neurons telling your hand and arm muscles to pull away from the heat.

The brain and body are interconnected. They use a system of cells to ping messages all around and through you. When it comes to emotions, the same networks are being used. Except instead of touching something hot and feeling burned, you may feel hurt or embarrassed or amused. Those feelings still tell neurons inside your head to fire off their signals, and those signals go all over your body and sometimes create physical sensations.

SWEATY PALMS & KNOCKING KNEES

You may not have thought about the connection between your body and your feelings before. But you've probably experienced many of these physical feelings. Each one can be paired with emotions.

Sweating It Out—It's really common to sweat when you feel nervous; the same can happen when you get angry (it's called heating up for a reason). Some people sweat on their face, especially along the forehead and above the upper lip. Others sweat in their armpits, behind their knees, or in the palms of their hands. And some sweat in all these places at once.

Flush Face—With some emotions, especially embarrassment, nervousness, and anger, blood flows to the face and you can start to look really red. Most people feel it, too, because their cheeks get warm. This is called having *flushed cheeks*, and it goes away once you begin to calm down or cool off.

Knocking Knees—For some people, nervousness causes their knees to shake up and down or back and forth; for others, the whole leg shakes. But some people never experience this.

Tensing Up—When the body gets ready for a fight or when it needs to defend itself against something heading its way, the muscles can get stiff and tense up. Some people clench their fists, others feel their shoulders lift up toward their ears, and others tighten their jaw.

Butterflies in the Belly—This feeling of fluttering in your stomach can happen when you are stressed or anxious; it can also happen when you are really excited. The feeling is caused by the stomach muscles temporarily changing the way they normally contract.

Thumping Heart—It is completely normal for the heart to thump super hard, super fast, or both when emotions (happy, nervous, sad, or angry ones) get turned up. The feeling in your chest can be so strong that it almost seems as though your heart could burst. But it won't, and when your feelings settle a bit, the thumping will mellow out as well.

Breathing Fast and Feeling Dizzy—Sometimes strong emotions can change the pace of your breathing, which can shift the amount of oxygen entering your body and getting to your brain. At times, this might make you feel dizzy. This sensation will pass, but it's best to sit down until it does.

Stomachache—Certain feelings, particularly negative ones, can cause stomach pains. This happens because the stomach's normal acid-making machinery (it's what helps us digest food) can go into high gear, making extra acid, which may feel like a burning sensation. Other times, the amount of acid is normal, but your emotions make you less hungry than usual, and with less food in your belly, the acid can cause some discomfort as well.

FIGHT or FLIGHT

What's the point of feeling like your heart is going to thump out of your chest or tensing up your muscles in a serious (sometimes seriously painful) way?

All those uncomfortable physical feelings are designed to keep you safe. Physical sensations help you pay attention and notice what's going on in your body and mind. When you're aware of how you're feeling, both physically and mentally, you can do something about it.

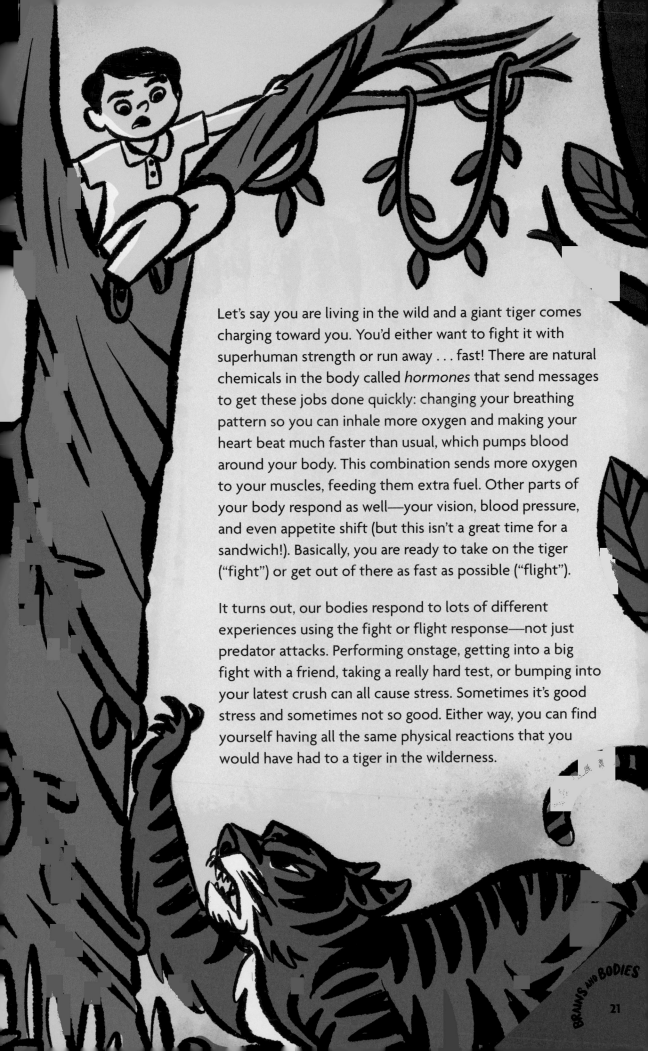

Let's say you are living in the wild and a giant tiger comes charging toward you. You'd either want to fight it with superhuman strength or run away . . . fast! There are natural chemicals in the body called *hormones* that send messages to get these jobs done quickly: changing your breathing pattern so you can inhale more oxygen and making your heart beat much faster than usual, which pumps blood around your body. This combination sends more oxygen to your muscles, feeding them extra fuel. Other parts of your body respond as well—your vision, blood pressure, and even appetite shift (but this isn't a great time for a sandwich!). Basically, you are ready to take on the tiger ("fight") or get out of there as fast as possible ("flight").

It turns out, our bodies respond to lots of different experiences using the fight or flight response—not just predator attacks. Performing onstage, getting into a big fight with a friend, taking a really hard test, or bumping into your latest crush can all cause stress. Sometimes it's good stress and sometimes not so good. Either way, you can find yourself having all the same physical reactions that you would have had to a tiger in the wilderness.

WHY do you CRY?

Crying can feel really embarrassing. Or annoying. Or inconvenient. Tears start to fall, and suddenly anyone who is looking your way can see that something's up. There are happy tears that come with unstoppable giggles. And there are sad tears that flow when you are down in the dumps.

Everyone cries: guys, girls, kids, adults, your teacher, your coach, even the president. You may not see it happen very often, but it helps to remember that all humans have feelings, and those feelings can trigger tears.

But why do people cry? The eyes make tears all day every day, but only in small enough amounts to keep your eyes moist, not enough to make you look like you're sobbing. When you cry, it's partly because the hormones that are connected to your sadness (or hysterical laughing) tell the eyes to make more tears. As you cry and hormone levels shift inside your body, you feel a sense of relief. Crying is also social—it cues other people that you may need help managing a situation.

Crying is absolutely fine. In fact, it's really healthy to cry every once in a while. Bottling up your emotions is never a great idea. But if you are crying a lot, check in with an adult who can help you figure out why.

Sometimes people will ask you why you are sad, but that doesn't always happen. In that case, go to someone—a friend, a parent, or a teacher—who can help you figure out the cause. At some point, you'll benefit from talking things through, because tears aren't the same as words. Crying can help release the immediate feeling, but to solve whatever is really bothering you, you need to talk about it.

A note about guys who cry: It's normal! In fact, it's healthy! Some guys think it's not "manly" to shed a tear, but that couldn't be further from the truth. Crying is human. More than that, letting out tears is part of being healthy and happy.

FEELING out of CONTROL

Emotions often happen in an instant. These reactions come so swiftly that they can make you feel as if you have no control.

Watching a funny movie, you might burst out laughing at a great joke. Seconds after your mom says you can't go hang out with your friends, you might feel like you want to yell or slam the door. When it's your turn to share a report with your entire class, your head might feel dizzy or your stomach queasy.

Remember that the brain is a collection of millions of neurons. Different areas in the brain have various functions—there are parts in charge of language, parts that command movement, and, yes, parts that are tied to emotion. Researchers continually learn more about how the brain works. For now, we know that one of the most important regions responsible for controlling how we feel and what we do in response is an area right in the middle of the brain called the *limbic system*. It is made up of a series of smaller brain parts, including the *amygdala*, two teeny almond-shaped areas that react particularly quickly. When a friend jumps out from around the corner and yells, "Boo!" thank your amygdala for feeling scared.

AMYGDALA

CONTROL

You already know that emotions result from a combination of neurons sending messages to one another and then out into the body. At the same time your legs are told to jump and your eyes shut (that "Boo!" was pretty scary, after all), your body is also instructed to release the hormones that get your heart pumping, your lungs inhaling, and your senses heightened. So, in a way, emotions are out of your immediate control—they are ruled by your brain and your body. But we can all learn over time how to better manage our feelings.

WHAT CAN you DO?

Just as certain parts of the brain are quick to respond with emotion, other parts take their time. Sometimes you'll react instantly and intensely. Or you might think about how you're feeling before you act. There's no one right way to experience your feelings, and it actually helps you manage your emotions when you balance immediate and slower responses.

The outer layer of the brain is called the *cerebrum*, and it weighs the facts of what happened, including your immediate reaction, before deciding what to do next. One part of the cerebrum, called the *prefrontal cortex*, is where choices are made very carefully. Here's where the brain can think through the consequences of an action. This part of the brain isn't fully developed until a person is at least 25 years old, explaining why kids and teens tend to act more impulsively than adults.

You can help control your mood by eating healthy foods, drinking lots of water, getting a good night's sleep, and exercising regularly. When you are hungry or tired, you may find yourself overreacting to a situation or snapping at someone when you wish you hadn't.

DELAYS

YOUR REACTION... 1-8 HRS.

PREFRONTAL CORTEX... 25 YEARS

Beyond healthy living, there are a whole bunch of strategies you can use to manage your feelings once they start to come out. Here are a few ideas:

Deep Breaths—In through the nose, out through the mouth, deeply and slowly. When you inhale for a count of four, hold for a count of four, and exhale for a count of four, you will often feel your body relax. The oxygen in these deep breaths helps fuel your cells, but just as important is the pace—calm breaths help a thumping heart slow down, and the very act of counting while you breathe will temporarily distract you from the situation that is causing you to feel so emotional.

Shoulders Down—Next time you are nervous or aggravated, take a second to drop your shoulders. Without you even realizing it, those shoulders may have lifted themselves up toward your ears. By relaxing your shoulders, you will also relax your neck muscles and likely let out a big exhale, all of which make you feel calmer and more in control.

Shake It Out—In the same way that it helps to relax your shoulders, shaking out your arms and legs can also give you the upper hand on your emotions. In fact, lots of times when the shoulders soften, the head shakes a little bit back and forth and the arms sway automatically. Relax your tense, flexed muscles by moving your body in any way that feels right to you: rolling your shoulders, hopping back and forth on one foot and then the other, opening your hands and then clenching them in a fist.

Move It!—Regular exercise is a great way to keep emotions balanced. Getting active will distract you, and when you move enough to break a sweat, your brain releases hormones that improve mood. Try doing something active the next time you are feeling really angry or sad or lonely or stressed. It can be anything, from running to yoga, joining a basketball game to, yes, dancing around your room. And by the way, if you are feeling out of control in a happy way—super giggly or silly—a workout can help here, too, by releasing energy.

Crack Up—Ever heard the expression "Laughter is the best medicine"? Laughing relaxes your muscles in the same way as shaking them out. And cracking up releases natural chemicals in your brain that work to reverse pain. You'll literally feel good when you laugh.

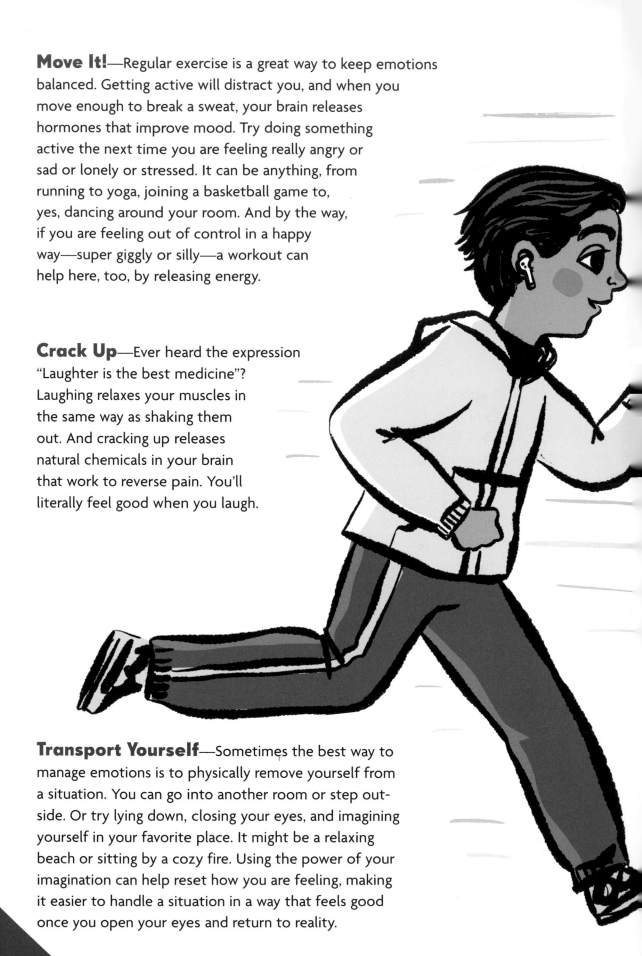

Transport Yourself—Sometimes the best way to manage emotions is to physically remove yourself from a situation. You can go into another room or step outside. Or try lying down, closing your eyes, and imagining yourself in your favorite place. It might be a relaxing beach or sitting by a cozy fire. Using the power of your imagination can help reset how you are feeling, making it easier to handle a situation in a way that feels good once you open your eyes and return to reality.

Feed Your Feelings Well—It's common for people to want to eat when their emotions are swirling. Some foods will make you feel better while others won't. Yes, a scoop of ice cream can turn a bad day into a better one, but a whole pint of ice cream does the opposite. In general, if you are feeling hungry when emotions are running high, try to feed yourself healthy foods. If you opt for a treat, keep the portions reasonable. Eating a bunch of junk can make big feelings feel even worse.

Don't Starve Your Feelings—Some people lose their appetite altogether when they get emotional. It's normal, and it's OK if you skip an occasional meal. But if your appetite decreases so much that you aren't eating enough food to nourish yourself, you'll start to feel worse. With too little food, energy levels drop and moods usually turn grumpy or sad. Keep yourself nourished and give your body some energy in the form of healthy food. If you find yourself eating too much or too little, talk to a trusted adult who can help you find better ways to cope with your feelings.

Rest and Reset—Sleep is key to wellness, including mood management. Try to get to bed at the same time every night and aim for at least 10 hours of sleep as a regular habit. When you are feeling particularly exhausted or emotional, you might want to sleep a little more, and that's OK. But sleeping too much over a period of time can be a sign that your emotions are starting to affect your body. Tell someone if you feel tired all the time, if you cannot get a good night's sleep, or if you are having serious trouble getting out of bed in the morning.

These are strategies to use in the moment, when you are trying to deal with an emotion as it is first appearing. There are other strategies covered a little later in the book that focus on managing emotions in the longer run, a few minutes or hours or even days after they first appear.

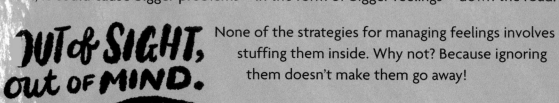

HOLDING *it all* IN

You might think that one way of handling your feelings is to ignore them, push them away, and pretend they don't exist. But this isn't going to help you move past them. In fact, it could cause bigger problems—in the form of bigger feelings—down the road.

OUT of SIGHT, out of MIND.

None of the strategies for managing feelings involves stuffing them inside. Why not? Because ignoring them doesn't make them go away!

If a friend says something hurtful, the only way to get past the anger or sadness you may be feeling involves talking to your friend and explaining that the comment wasn't OK. It can seem easier just to keep the feeling inside, especially because it's a lot of work to talk things out with someone else.

Think of feelings like the bubbles inside a can of soda. Sitting still, there are just a few bubbles lining the side walls. But shake up that liquid, and suddenly the bubbles multiply, the pressure inside increases, and when you pop the top, foamy liquid sprays out all over. In the same way, if you stuff down your feelings, you might be fine when everything else is going your way. But as soon as something shakes you up—you don't do well on a test in school, you lose a big game, you get in a fight with someone you really care about—then everything bubbles up to the surface. Open your mouth and you might say something you regret.

Expressing feelings can be difficult for anyone, but especially for guys who think that being "manly" means being tough and never showing anyone how they feel. This idea of what makes a man is completely false. Ask any man you know: your dad, your coach, your favorite family friend. Most will tell you how much better they feel when they let their feelings out, even when those feelings seem overwhelming or come with tears.

FIGURING it OUT 3

It can be a lot of work to sort out why you feel a certain way. First, you need to recognize what's happening inside. Then you must connect it with a reason—what else is going on that's stirring up this emotion? If you don't take these two steps, it is hard to resolve the feeling. You don't want to stay sad or mad forever. If you're having trouble figuring out your feelings, talk with a friend or adult you can trust.

WHAT'S YOUR REACTION?

We're all different, from the color of our hair to the sports we like to play. Our feelings are different, too. This is why a bunch of people can watch the same movie, but each person will have a different reaction to it—like when you find something hilariously funny but no one else even cracks a smile.

Have you ever been surprised by your reaction to a situation? It happens. You might think something will be no big deal, but in the moment, you tear up. Or it could be the opposite: Something you anticipate nervously goes off without a hitch and not a speck of worry. Emotions can vary, both in type (happy vs. sad) and intensity (overpowering vs. no big deal). How you feel depends on your personality, your past experiences, and the exact circumstances around you at the moment. In other words, it's totally normal to have different types of reactions—different from your friends and even different from the way you felt before.

Circle the answer that best describes how a person might feel in these situations.

Your best friend is acting like a clown at school, making you the butt of the joke. You feel . . .

a. amused. She's so funny!

b. embarrassed. You hate being the center of attention.

c. annoyed. Why is she always making fun of you?

d. offended. That joke isn't even funny and it hurts your feelings.

Your sister is talking loudly with her friends while you are trying to study. You're feeling . . .

a. calm. They are actually easy to tune out.

b. slightly annoyed. They're being kind of rude.

c. anxious. What if you can't focus long enough to finish your homework?

d. furious. She and her friends are ruining your study time!

You are cut from the basketball team, and the rest of your friends made it. You feel . . .

a. surprised. You were sure you'd make the team.

b. disappointed. But maybe now's the time to try something new.

c. embarrassed. You thought you were just as good as the other guys.

d. angry. The tryout process seemed unfair.

You are invited to a friend's birthday party at the new go-cart racing place. You feel . . .

a. excited. You've always wanted to try go-carting. Looks like so much fun!

b. nervous. You've never been go-carting. You don't want to look inexperienced.

c. shy. Who else will be there that you know?

d. happy. It feels so good to be included.

Answers

Every feeling in these situations is appropriate. Your emotional reaction depends on your personality, and you might even feel a mix of feelings in certain situations. A person can react lots of different ways. Even if you are a relaxed, go-with-the-flow guy, you still might have moments of being really upset or excited. Or maybe you're a guy who tends to respond with more ups and downs. You are still entitled to have moments when you react to a situation like it's a nothing sandwich.

SITTING with your FEELINGS

You might not be able to completely control your emotions when they first appear, and that's normal. After your initial reaction, try to sit with those feelings for a little while, even if it feels uncomfortable. With time, you may be able to understand your emotions more clearly and handle them with more grace.

Part of sorting through how you feel is giving yourself time. Remember that the brain reacts to situations instantly. But feelings grow and change, too. Have you ever been jealous of your best friend spending time with someone else? Maybe when he told you he had other plans, you didn't really care, but later, sitting at home alone, you started to feel jealous. And maybe you even got mad. But the next day, when you saw each other, your friendship was back to normal and you had pretty much forgotten about the day before.

When you sit with your feelings—even strong feelings—you give them a chance to shift around. And after a few minutes (or sometimes hours or days), they become steady and less overwhelming. Jealousy may change to anger, which might change to feeling bland, almost like feeling nothing at all. But jealousy could also change to anger and stick there. Once feelings settle down, then you can deal with them. This is why giving yourself time with an emotion can be very helpful in learning how to manage it.

But be careful. If you are giving yourself time to sit with your feelings, don't let that be an excuse for not dealing with them. When you don't deal with your emotions, you're just shoving them into an invisible backpack, and if you do this enough, that backpack gets seriously heavy. You will find yourself carrying around the weight of unresolved feelings. After a while, you may have trouble dealing with almost any emotion in a way that feels good. So sure, take a little time. But don't put it off forever.

Timing tip: Let's say you sat on things for a while and you've decided it's finally time to talk them through. Pick your moment carefully. Don't start a big talk when time is limited, like right before you are meant to go to bed or as you are walking into a class. Talking things through might take more time and energy than you expect.

STRATEGIES for SORTING things OUT

Once you've figured out how you're feeling, the next step is to create a plan that will help you deal with your emotions.

In the same way that we all have our own emotional reactions, we also all have unique ways of figuring out how we feel and why. How you deal with your feelings might be very different from how a friend or another family member deals with his. That's totally fine—there's no right way.

No matter how you go about sorting through your emotions, as you grow up, you'll figure out certain ways that work best for you. If you haven't gotten there quite yet, the next few pages have a bunch of ideas that might help. You can also watch how others get in touch with their feelings and try those ideas yourself. We never stop learning from the people around us, including lessons about how to manage our emotions.

HOPE

ANGER

When you really start looking around, you will see good and bad strategies. The people who shove their feelings away may appear to handle everything that comes their way, but deep down they aren't necessarily that happy. The ones who allow themselves to feel their emotions and manage them in a healthy way tend to have more balance and more joy in their lives, even if they show sadness, frustration, or fear from time to time.

WORRY

CALM

THRILL

envy

WORRY

REGRET

OURAGE

JOY

FEAR

HUMOR

EXCITEMEN

FRUSTRATION

WRITING things DOWN

WHY??? CAN'T EXPLAIN it

Journaling means writing your thoughts out, though you don't have to write in paragraphs or even full sentences. Single words are just fine. Use whatever language helps you sort through a situation. And you don't need an official journal—a piece of paper works! Pulling your thoughts out of your head will help you understand them, and those big feelings you have won't feel like they control you.

List-making is kind of like journaling but organized differently. Here you write down your thoughts with a goal of figuring out the answer to a specific question, such as what are the pros and cons of yelling right now? Or when have I felt like this before, and what did I do then? Or you could list "Things that make me feel _____" (fill in the blank with your current emotion). Some lists have solutions; others just have feelings.

Drawing or **doodling** works well for some people. Or try creating a map connecting how you feel with where the feeling came from and what you can do to deal with that feeling.

I FEEL boxed IN←

SCHOOL HOME

THIS IS FINE.

MOM DAD

SISTER

SO MUCH

NO TIME

LOSING IT

✓ PROS:
↑ RELIEF!
HONESTY!

🔍 CONS:
↓ REGRET
embarrassing

ALEX
IS NEVER IN TROUBLE
WHY is IT ALWAYS ME?

You can always combine strategies. Try writing your feelings and then imagine a conversation you might have with a trusted friend, playing out the different ways it might go. Or show your journal to someone you trust and ask for his advice on what to do from here. But keep your journal in a safe place because it's filled with private thoughts. These aren't secrets, but they belong only to you. If you leave your journal somewhere that others can easily find it, you won't get to choose who reads it and who doesn't.

YOUR PRIVATE THOUGHTS are YOURS.

TALKING THINGS OUT

Talking to someone you trust is always a great strategy, but it's especially helpful when you are trying to work through an emotion. Amazingly, people who know you well might be able to identify how you feel before you can. They might ask "What's wrong?" before you ever had a chance to tell them you were upset. While it might be annoying that someone else seems to know you better than you know yourself, turning to parents, siblings, or friends who know you well is almost always a good idea.

Choosing the right person to talk to is key. If you are trying to sort through feelings around how a friend treated you, it might be best to talk to someone who can listen to your side and then help you see the other person's perspective, too. Sometimes adults are better in this role; other times they don't get it quite as well as a friend your age would. Remember, though, to always go to a person who has your best interest in mind.

Some conversations should go straight to an adult, particularly concerns that involve your or someone else's safety. Trusted adults who you can lean on—and talk to—when you need help sorting things out include parents, other family members, teachers, faith-community leaders, doctors, school counselors, and therapists.

Keep things private. Yes, pick a person or two to bounce your feelings off of, but don't vent to your entire class or team. That just creates drama. Besides, your goal here is to sort out how you feel about a situation, not to make other people who were involved feel bad.

Because it's so helpful to get advice from other people, take a moment to write a list of the ones you can go to when you are stuck. And then lean on these people for advice. But don't forget to share the good stuff with them as well! Just because someone is great at helping you with a worry or a concern doesn't mean he shouldn't hear about your joys and successes.

Dear GRANDPA, SOME really great stuff is HAPPENING. I met a NEW FRIEND and

the VOICE INSIDE

4

Does it feel like you can hear your thoughts? They don't actually make noises, but it can certainly seem like there's a conversation going on in your head. That's the voice inside you, and here's how to interpret what it's saying.

LISTENING IN

No one has a single inner voice. We have different thoughts going through our minds all the time. How they "sound" depends on how we feel in a situation.

It's a weird thing to think about your inner voice, but it's there all the time. Even as you are reading this page, the words in front of you run through your mind like a conversation that no one else can hear (that is, unless you are reading out loud, in which case everyone nearby can hear!).

Once you become aware of this "voice," you can begin to appreciate its mood. That's right— the voice inside can be happy or sad, snappy or forgiving, guilty or generous. It's often the first clue to how you feel. If a kid in your class walks up to you and says, "Loser!" that voice inside might reply, "No I'm not. What a jerk!" Or if you're having a hard day, that voice might say, "He's right. I am a loser." When you listen to how you really talk to yourself, you can learn a lot about how you're feeling.

Your inner voice is so powerful that it can determine how you behave toward other people. That's why it's important to do more than listen to what your mind is saying. Try to figure out how you're feeling and why you are responding the way you are. When you understand why you are thinking or acting a certain way, you'll be able to make adjustments in your behaviors.

Your inner voice often reflects your *mind-set*— or the way you approach a new idea or situation. Your mindset is your attitude. If you think you are good at something—could be math, could be running, could be cracking jokes—you are more likely to try to excel at that thing than if you think you can't do it. And the more you try, the more likely you are to eventually succeed. This is called an *open mindset* or a growth mindset. Its opposite is a *fixed mindset*, where you are certain about the way something will go and that opinion isn't changing. Your inner voice often reflects your mindset. So when you decide to shift your mindset, the tone of your inner voice will change as well.

THE CIRCLE of EMOTIONS

Ever had a really bad day when everything seemed to go wrong? Or a really good one when it felt like luck was on your side? This happens because your emotions, thoughts, and behavior are all interconnected.

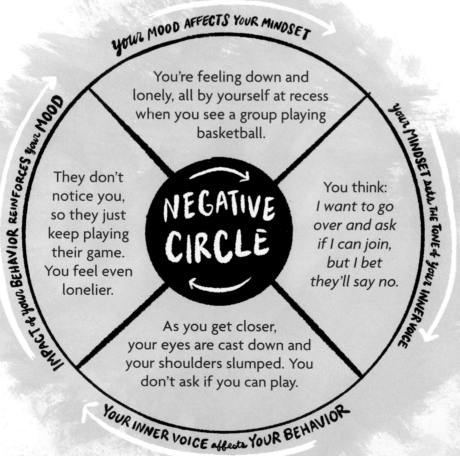

POSITIVE CIRCLE

your MOOD AFFECTS YOUR MINDSET

your MINDSET sets THE TONE of your INNER VOICE

YOUR INNER VOICE affects YOUR BEHAVIOR

IMPACT of your BEHAVIOR REINFORCES your MOOD

You are in a great mood and hanging out alone at recess when you see a group of guys playing basketball.

You think: *I should go over and ask if I can join.*

You approach the group with a smile and ask to play.

They pass you the ball, and you jump into the game. You feel even happier.

NEGATIVE CIRCLE

your MOOD AFFECTS YOUR MINDSET

your MINDSET sets THE TONE of your INNER VOICE

YOUR INNER VOICE affects YOUR BEHAVIOR

IMPACT of your BEHAVIOR REINFORCES your MOOD

You're feeling down and lonely, all by yourself at recess when you see a group playing basketball.

You think: *I want to go over and ask if I can join, but I bet they'll say no.*

As you get closer, your eyes are cast down and your shoulders slumped. You don't ask if you can play.

They don't notice you, so they just keep playing their game. You feel even lonelier.

CHANGING the CIRCLE of EMOTIONS

No one is stuck in a circle of emotion forever. You can shift your mindset and break the cycle.

You have the power to flip negative thoughts to positive ones because you have the power to shift your attitude, mindset, and behavior.

To do this, you need to . . .

1. recognize how you are feeling.

2. decide how you want to feel instead.

3. figure out what it will take to get from 1 to 2.

HOW to CHANGE the CIRCLE

YOUR MOOD AFFECTS YOUR MINDSET

You're feeling down and lonely, all by yourself at recess when you see a group playing basketball.

POINT of INTERVENTION

YOUR MINDSET sets THE TONE of YOUR INNER VOICE

You think: *I want to go over and ask if I can join, but I bet they'll say no.*

POINT of INTERVENTION

YOUR INNER VOICE affects YOUR BEHAVIOR

As you get closer, your eyes are cast down and your shoulders slumped. You don't ask if you can play.

POINT of INTERVENTION

IMPACT of YOUR BEHAVIOR REINFORCES YOUR MOOD

They don't notice you, so they just keep playing their game. You feel even lonelier.

POINT of INTERVENTION

FLIP to THE POSITIVE cycle

Try a little harder, because they are in the middle of a game after all. Clear your throat or wave and say "Hey."

But no matter what happens, know that you're courageous to put yourself out there. Be proud. Next time, this won't be so hard.

FLIP to THE POSITIVE cycle

If you recognize that you're feeling lonely and you don't like how that feels, make a decision to change it by finding someone to hang out with.

FLIP to THE POSITIVE cycle

Choose to straighten your spine, look at the other kids, and find the courage to ask if you can join.

FLIP to THE POSITIVE cycle

Disagree with your inner voice, because assuming what other people will say is just a guess . . . and sometimes that guess is wrong.

TACKLING NEGATIVE THOUGHTS

Sometimes it's not so easy to shift your emotions, especially when you feel really down in the dumps.

A mountain that's insurmountable is one that's impossible to climb. Emotions can feel insurmountable, too. This is particularly true when feelings are negative. What should you do when you get down on yourself? Here are some examples of negative thoughts and strategies for turning them around:

THE VOICE INSIDE

Hating how you look: Both guys and girls can feel insecure about their body shape or their height or the features on their faces. This is totally normal, especially in the tween and teen years. It is usually easier to see the things you don't like about yourself, particularly when you are staring in the mirror. Some tips:

• Walk away from the mirror!

• Try not to compare yourself with others.

• Pick at least one feature about yourself that you do like and let that balance out the thing you are feeling down about at the moment.

Check out how different you look when you stand up straight, smile, and think about yourself positively. Seriously, this is what you should practice in front of a mirror, not hunting for zits.

Feeling dumb: We all feel stupid from time to time. We all say things we wish we hadn't or give an answer that's wrong because we didn't know the right one. It can feel humiliating. Some tips:

• Laugh it off.

• Remember that everyone makes mistakes, even people who are really smart.

• Learn for the next time—if you are so busy being embarrassed about not knowing, you might not be able to focus on the right answer.

It's OK to cringe because you messed up on a test, lost a big match, or said something that caused drama. What's not OK is to beat yourself up mentally because making mistakes is how you learn.

THE VOICE INSIDE

Being the last one: Feeling left out is uncomfortable. Maybe all your friends are allowed to play a video game that your parents won't let you download. Or maybe a group is hanging out and you weren't included. Ever been the last one picked for a team? None of this stuff feels good. Some tips:

• If you've been excluded from an activity, find something more fun to do.

• Be sensitive to the next guy who is left out . . . and try to include him if you can.

• Think about the activities or events you have been invited to or the privileges your parents have given you ahead of some of your friends. You are probably not always the last at everything.

WHO can you TRUST?

Sometimes you'll want to share your feelings with someone else. Other times, you'll want to talk through a situation so that you can understand how you feel. Either way, how do you decide whom to open up to?

Choosing the right person to confide in is a big deal. No matter what you are feeling, the person you go to might influence what you do next, and this influence can be stronger when your emotions are riding high. So how do you choose whom to confide in?

A parent or trusted adult will always have your back—their job is to keep you safe and healthy, and because they are older, they have gained wisdom from life experience.

A close friend your own age may understand parts of your life without you having to explain everything, especially if you share the same friends or go to the same school.

A sibling or cousin might know you in ways others don't . . . and they might be able to offer advice that others wouldn't think of.

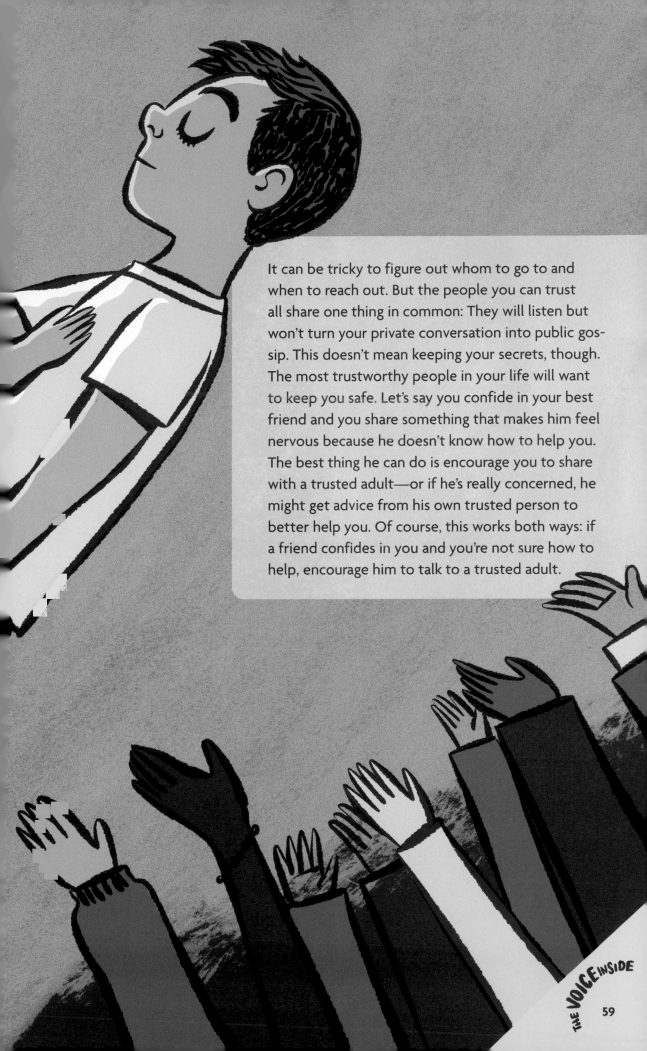

It can be tricky to figure out whom to go to and when to reach out. But the people you can trust all share one thing in common: They will listen but won't turn your private conversation into public gossip. This doesn't mean keeping your secrets, though. The most trustworthy people in your life will want to keep you safe. Let's say you confide in your best friend and you share something that makes him feel nervous because he doesn't know how to help you. The best thing he can do is encourage you to share with a trusted adult—or if he's really concerned, he might get advice from his own trusted person to better help you. Of course, this works both ways: if a friend confides in you and you're not sure how to help, encourage him to talk to a trusted adult.

5 I FEEL...

SAFE CORNER

JEALOUSY LANE

the REGRE a ROUN

Once you've identified an emotion, you are in much more control over how you can react to it. There are solid strategies for turning around particular emotions. Planning ahead for how to handle a feeling when it pops up makes that feeling much less overwhelming.

ANXIETY EXPRESS

GRIEVING GROVE

ANGER AVE

CONFIDENCE BOULEVARD →

the PLAN

WAITING ZONE

I FEEL...

I'M SCARED

Fear comes in lots of forms. There's the scary-movie type, the deep-worry type, and the type that comes from not knowing what to expect. Everyone is scared of something . . . and some people are scared of lots of things. Everyone has the power to manage his fears.

The feeling: Being scared can feel like a pit in your stomach. Your heart might race. You might get dizzy or sweaty. You might start breathing quickly. Or you might squeeze your eyes shut to avoid seeing something that will freak you out.

The physical reactions that go along with fear depend on the situation you're in. If you are on your bike and about to wipe out, you might shut your eyes at the very last second and even hold your breath. But if you are in front of your class about to give a presentation, your eyes are likely to stay open and your breathing may become quicker. Fear looks different for everyone and in every circumstance.

I FEEL...

SOME SCARY SITUATIONS

- A big change in the family structure, like parents splitting up or a sibling moving away

- Speaking up in school, whether in class or in front of the whole student body

- A runaway imagination, often thinking about the worst thing that can happen in a situation

- Trying something new, particularly when other people have been doing that same thing for a while or when others are watching

- Being left alone, even when you know an adult will be coming back or someone will join you soon

I FEEL...

63

If your heart is racing or you are breathing fast, take a few very slow, deep breaths in and out. Closing your eyes while doing this can really help (unless closing your eyes is dangerous at that moment). After a few seconds of taking control of your breathing, you will feel your heartbeat slow a little bit. Your mind might even feel clearer.

If your hands are shaking, try opening and closing them, clenching your fists and then stretching your fingers wide. Or shake them out at your wrists. This moves blood into your hands and relaxes the muscles.

If your stomach is hurting and you have a burning feeling in your throat, this could be caused by acids that normally help digest food but can get pumped into the stomach during moments of fear. If there's water available, sip on that. A little bland food, such as a cracker, can also help.

If you're dizzy, sit down! The last thing you want to do is pass out. Just take a moment in a chair—this will help blood get back up to your brain, which will help the dizziness go away. Drinking water also helps.

AAAHH!!!

I'M SURE THE KILLER IS GONE. I'LL GO LOOK OUTSIDE...

If you are freaked out by something you are watching, turn it off or leave the room. If you are reading something that is scaring you, close the book and put it away.

I FEEL...

65

I'M ANXIOUS

Anxiety is the feeling of stress even without the stressor being right there. For instance, if you have a big test, you might feel stressed out studying beforehand. But once it's over, if the feeling of worry doesn't go away, that's anxiety. The test is done, but your emotion is not.

The feeling: Anxiety can feel a lot like fear—racing heart, rapid breathing, and stomachache all go along with being anxious. But anxiety usually stretches out over a much longer time than fear, so the body's response may feel a little less intense but last a whole lot longer. Some people will pick or bite their nails when they are anxious; others pull on their hair. Some people clench their jaw without even realizing it. After a while, they might develop pain inside the cheek or in the form of a headache. Some anxious kids have trouble falling asleep at night.

These days, kids are pretty aware of anxiety. Teachers talk about stress management at school, and parents, coaches, doctors, and others might suggest self-care, which includes all the things you can do to take care of your mind and body—stuff like exercising, eating well, getting lots of sleep, and meditating.

Situations that can cause kids to feel anxious (you'll notice that some of these overlap with the causes of fear):

School workload and worries about grades

Sports stress, including the feeling that you need to practice more and more to keep up with teammates

Getting into an accident or finding out you have an illness

The future, whether it's the job you'll have, health issues you might face, or topics in the news, such as climate change

A big change in family structure, like parents splitting up or a sibling moving away

Being left alone, even when you know an adult will come back

I FEEL...

If you have trouble sleeping, try distracting yourself by reading or listening to a book. Or learn meditation strategies that you can use when you get into bed. Some kids find that it really helps to drink warm herbal tea or warm milk; others like a bath or a shower right before bedtime.

YUCK

If you bite your nails, try putting a special, bad-tasting nail treatment on your fingers, because as soon as your hands enter your mouth, they will taste so gross you won't want them in there! If you are a nail-picker, you could try putting bandages or tape on the nails you pick. But be sure to remove the tape after a day or two and let the area air out for a while.

If you get headaches, talk to your doctor about what you can do to reduce them. Your doctor can help you make sure that there isn't another reason for your headaches that might be fixed another way.

If your stomach hurts, take a look at what you are eating and how much—sometimes people don't eat well (or at all!) when they are anxious, and this makes the acid levels in their stomach rise, causing a cramping or burning pain.

Regardless of how your body responds to anxiety, the very best way to feel better is to get to the root of the problem. If you can identify what is making you anxious, and then if you can either fix it or talk about it until your stress goes away, the physical feelings will probably disappear, too.

I'M SO JEALOUS

Jealousy, or envy, is the feeling when you wish something that is happening to someone else were happening to you. It can make you feel inadequate. And it's completely natural to feel jealous some of the time, but it can make us feel—or act—badly.

The feeling: Jealousy usually feels like a knot in your stomach mixed with a bit of sadness. Sometimes there's anger thrown in there as well. Compared to some of the other emotions discussed in this book, jealousy doesn't have quite as many physical sensations associated with it. But for many people, jealousy or envy causes them to have a bunch of thoughts about another person that aren't so nice, because being jealous goes hand in hand with feeling like something is unfair.

You might feel jealous of another kid if he's . . .

- popular, or has a group of friends and never seems lonely.

- successful—this can be in the classroom or on the field or playing video games.

- good looking, or if he doesn't seem to be struggling with the physical thing that drives you crazy about yourself.

- well-off—financial differences are a big source of envy among people.

- relaxed, or at least not stressed over the things that you worry about.

I FEEL...

71

If you get angry when someone else gets attention, calm yourself down by taking deep breaths and chilling out.

If you get down when someone else gets an A but you don't, choose to look on the bright side and figure out how to do better the next time.

I FEEL...

72

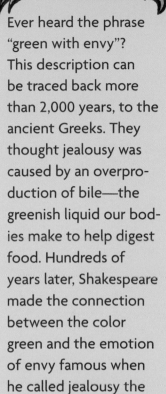

ME! MINE! MORE!

Ever heard the phrase "green with envy"? This description can be traced back more than 2,000 years, to the ancient Greeks. They thought jealousy was caused by an overproduction of bile—the greenish liquid our bodies make to help digest food. Hundreds of years later, Shakespeare made the connection between the color green and the emotion of envy famous when he called jealousy the "green-eyed monster."

If you can't handle it when someone else wins, excuse yourself from the situation, because being a sore loser won't make you feel any better and it often makes other people uncomfortable. But don't storm off and be all dramatic about it.

I FEEL...

I'VE been DISRESPECTED

Disrespect comes in many forms, like bullying, teasing, mocking, shaming, and being ignored. It can be hard to handle these moments because you need to have lots of confidence to stand up for yourself or someone else.

The feeling: When someone disrespects you, you might feel hurt. This pain usually comes from shame or embarrassment, which can make you literally cringe (clenched teeth, squinting eyes, shoulders up by your ears). There are times when disrespect can bring out sadness—with or without tears—or fear—with or without a thumping heartbeat and shaking knees. Some people feel alone when they are disrespected, particularly when they think other people believe what is being said about them. They can isolate themselves because they don't want to be bullied again, which can make emotions feel even more intense.

Disrespect happens in person and online. In fact, it's easier for a bully to say something nasty without looking another person in the eye. This is why it is so common for people to be on the receiving end of online teasing or torment.

You might feel disrespected if you . . .

- overhear someone saying something negative about you.

- get shut out of a conversation or left out of a group.

- become the butt of a joke.

- try to apologize but the other person won't accept your explanation.

Without even knowing it, you might do some disrespectful things, too, like . . .

- ignoring your parents when they ask you to help around the house.

- laughing at someone else when he wasn't joking around.

- not looking someone in the eyes when he speaks to you. Making eye contact can be tough, but it can seem disrespectful if you don't.

If you say something in class and everyone laughs, you might try laughing along with them. Sometimes not taking yourself so seriously allows you to let go of negative feelings more easily.

If you try to have a conversation with someone but he tunes you out, you might try telling him that the conversation is important to you, and it hurts that he isn't listening.

I FEEL...

If you read comments about yourself online or on a text thread, show them to a trusted adult who can help you manage this form of bullying.

If you're the one not listening to a friend when he's trying to share something with you, apologize. We can all feel disrespected, but we can also be the ones doing the disrespecting.

I FEEL...

I'M ANGRY

Everyone gets mad. But no one likes how it feels to be angry or to be the one receiving the anger. There are ways to manage this emotion so that you don't hit a boiling point.

The feeling: Anger is one of those feelings that can be so strong that it's hard to describe it with words. Maybe you clench your fists or your teeth (or both). Some people feel their heart racing when they get mad; others feel like the world around them goes silent and all they can hear are the thoughts inside their head. You might start to feel warm, your face might flush red, you might even sweat a little—in fact, being mad is often described with words associated with heat. And as anger goes away, we say we are cooling off.

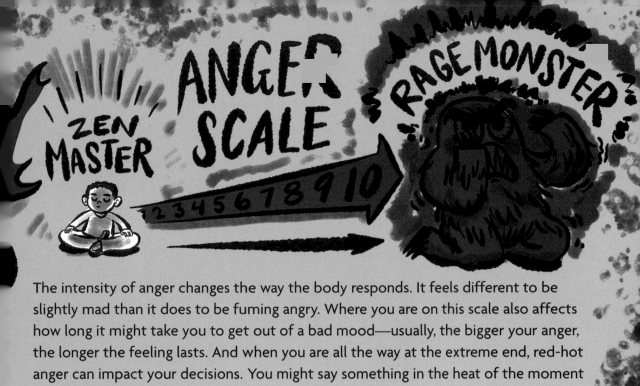

ANGER SCALE

ZEN MASTER

RAGE MONSTER

1 2 3 4 5 6 7 8 9 10

The intensity of anger changes the way the body responds. It feels different to be slightly mad than it does to be fuming angry. Where you are on this scale also affects how long it might take you to get out of a bad mood—usually, the bigger your anger, the longer the feeling lasts. And when you are all the way at the extreme end, red-hot anger can impact your decisions. You might say something in the heat of the moment that you really regret later.

Things that make people angry include . . . well, all sorts of things. Someone can say, do, show, repeat, or believe something that you don't agree with, sometimes so much so that you feel mad about it. Anger can come from watching or reading about something that is happening to someone else, too.

I FEEL...

When you are slightly bothered by something—just a little mad—you might be able to take a breath, choose your words, and explain how you feel.

When you are a bit angrier, you might want to walk away for a moment so that you can cool down before you come back and share your feelings.

Sometimes writing how you feel is a great way to let the anger out. But don't press send right away! Avoid sharing an angry note until some time has passed—once your mindset has shifted to a more positive place, reread what you wrote. You may not even want to share what you wrote. If you do, make sure your words reflect what you mean to say. Remember, words in the heat of the moment can cause bigger conflicts and create bigger feelings that can be harder to deal with later.

I FEEL...

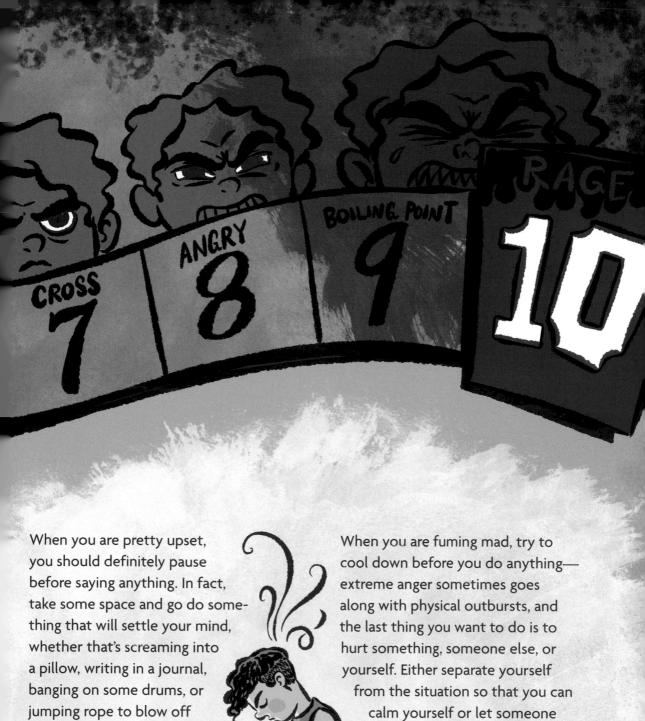

CROSS
7

ANGRY
8

BOILING POINT
9

RAGE
10

When you are pretty upset, you should definitely pause before saying anything. In fact, take some space and go do something that will settle your mind, whether that's screaming into a pillow, writing in a journal, banging on some drums, or jumping rope to blow off steam.

When you are fuming mad, try to cool down before you do anything—extreme anger sometimes goes along with physical outbursts, and the last thing you want to do is to hurt something, someone else, or yourself. Either separate yourself from the situation so that you can calm yourself or let someone else help you vent your anger in a safe place.

I FEEL...

I'M LONELY

The weird thing about loneliness is that you don't have to be alone to feel it. Feeling lonely is really about feeling isolated. If you are on your own, you might experience loneliness, but if you are left out of a group activity or an inside joke—even if your friends are right there next to you—loneliness can creep up as well.

The feeling: Being lonely often feels a lot like being sad. Some people describe a pit in their stomach or a lump in their throat; others will get teary. Body language can change when people feel lonely: the shoulders round, the back curves, the chin hangs down, and eyes are downcast. When a person feels positive and confident, he might stand up straight and stick out his chest and make direct eye contact. Being lonely can make you want to do the opposite of that and just curl in on yourself.

Being lonely doesn't necessarily mean you are alone—it means you feel alone. If you were stranded on a desert island and had no one to keep you company, you'd probably feel pretty lonely (by the way, the chance of that happening is basically zero). But you can feel just as isolated if you are with a group of friends and are completely left out of their conversation, or if you are at home with your parents but they are fighting. Some people describe feeling invisible, like no one can see them. This can cause them to pull back from a group, sending signals to the others that they aren't interested in being part of whatever is going on.

You might feel lonely if . . .

- you are away from home, in a new environment like a sleepover or at camp.

- you are sitting alone during lunch at school.

- your friends make a plan that doesn't include you.

- your parents live in separate houses and you are staying with one but missing the other.

- you are sitting on the bench while everyone else is playing in the game.

I FEEL....

When you are completely alone and feeling isolated because there are no people around, try distracting yourself by playing a card game or an instrument or watching a funny movie to pass the time.

When you are feeling lonely at night, especially when you are not sleeping in your own bed, call the person you miss to say good night. If you can't sleep, try reading a book.

I FEEL

When you are with your friends but feeling left out of their conversation, try to muster the courage to jump in or ask someone what you missed—if you are curious in a positive way, there's a higher chance you'll be included than if you look miserable or if you demand to know what's going on.

When you are out of the game while everyone else is playing, find another kid who is also out and strike up a conversation.

When an old friend moves on and makes new pals but you really miss how the two of you used to hang around, tell him how you feel—he may not realize you feel left out.

I FEEL...

I'M really SAD

Sadness is another emotion we've all felt. Like other feelings, there are different degrees of being sad—when a person is so down that his heart feels broken or he's having trouble getting through his day, he needs help.

The feeling: Most people describe the feeling of sadness as emptiness in the body's core—the sense that there's a giant pit in your stomach or a hole in your heart. When a person is down, his energy can be low, too. That can mean that extremely sad people have trouble motivating themselves to do their work or connect with friends, and some even have difficulty getting out of bed in the morning.

When you feel sad, it can be tough to enjoy anything going on around you. A funny show that always makes you laugh suddenly doesn't appeal to you. Or an activity that would normally be super fun—a game or a shopping trip or just hanging around with your friends—is of no interest.

There are lots of reasons to feel sad. And depending on the reason, the way you experience your sadness will change. Sometimes you might cry when you are sad, but other times you will just want to be quiet or alone. Both are normal. It's also normal for different people to have unique reactions, so what makes you sad might not upset your closest friend. It's important to recognize this, so that when the roles are reversed and he's the one who is down but you're not, you can be sensitive to his emotions.

LOVE AT HOME

Things that make people sad include:

- Getting a bad grade in school

- Losing a big game

- Living with conflict, like fighting family members

- Having to deal with being sick—your own illness or that of a family member or close friend

- Losing a loved one (more on that in the next section about grief)

- Getting into a big fight with someone you care about

- Breaking a rule and feeling like you have let your parents—and yourself—down

I FEEL...

The steps for managing sadness are basic healthy-living skills, but these skills become even more important when you are feeling really low:

Self-care: Eat healthfully and get exercise—doing both of these things fuels your body, while eating lots of junk and just lying around make you feel worse.

Let it out: If you are feeling sad enough to cry, then let the tears flow. We all feel better when we release an emotion, and there is nothing weak about crying.

Get outside: Fresh air makes everyone feel better. So does a little sunshine.

ZZZ

Sleep: Getting a good night's sleep makes a big difference in resetting your mood. If you cannot sleep or cannot get out of bed in the morning, it's time to ask someone for help.

HEALTHY Living

GOOD BOOKS

CONNECT!

Connect with friends: They can help you by talking through your sadness or by talking about all sorts of other things to distract you—and friends really want to help.

Steer clear of negativity: Surround yourself with people who love and support you, and stay away from people who make you feel insecure.

I FEEL...

What's depression?

It's deep sadness that requires help from a professional. Sometimes medication is also needed to fix this type of sadness. It can be hard for a person to know whether he is depressed—often friends and family members see things that we don't see in ourselves. The list below describes feelings that can go along with depression. If you have any of these, talk to your parents or a trusted adult to get help. You can move beyond these feelings.

- Deep sadness lasting a long time (more than a few days)

- Difficulty falling asleep or staying asleep every night

- Difficulty getting out of bed in the morning—not just feeling lazy, but really not being able to face the day

- Constantly feeling angry or irritable

- Unable to enjoy things that are usually fun or exciting for you

- Stomachaches or headaches that don't get better

- Unable to eat or eating out of control

- Feeling badly about yourself in lots of ways or all the time

- Thinking a lot about death or thinking about suicide*

- Thinking about hurting yourself or someone else*

* If you have any thoughts about harming yourself or others, you need to talk to a trusted adult right away so that you can get the help you need to stay safe.

Lean on adults: Parents or others who care for you might not know something's wrong and cannot help unless you share.

Communicate: Share your feelings so that you can process them and move past them. This might mean talking to someone or writing down why you feel sad.

I FEEL...

89

I'M GRIEVING

Grief is a specific type of sadness that comes from losing someone special to you. When a person or a family pet dies, we feel grief. When a close friend moves away, we feel it, too.

The feeling: Grief is a combination of sadness mixed with other emotions, especially anger, fear, and loneliness. There are days when all these emotions come out at once, which can feel overwhelming. Other times, the emotions take turns, so you might get angry with your mom and then storm away just to feel lonely in your room.

Everyone grieves differently. As you grow up, your grieving will change, too. That's because you gain life experience as you mature, which shifts how you handle grief. When you were younger, you might not have understood the feeling of loss the way you do now—grief is one of those emotions that can get more intense as you get older. But with age, you'll also get better at knowing how to handle it.

SPOT

Most of the time, people deal with their grief in steps. The process goes like this:

STEP 1
Denial: At first, you might not want to think about the loss at all. You might even try to forget it happened.

STEP 2
Anger: You get mad about the loss and you might take it out on other people (frustration) or on yourself (anxiety).

STEP 3
Bargaining: This is a stage where you try to make sense of the loss. Why did that person have to die? Or why did my best friend need to move so far away?

STEP 4
Sadness or depression: You let yourself feel the loss by getting sad, which allows you to express the emotion rather than keeping it bottled up inside.

STEP 5
Acceptance: You might still miss them, but you know you are going to be OK. You will always have memories. If the loss isn't permanent, you can find new ways to connect.

While each of these stages is normal, experiencing any one of them for a long time or in the extreme can create more problems. For instance, getting a little angry is understandable, but if you yell at everyone in your house or if you lose your temper with your friends, people are not going to want to be around you, even when they know you are going through a tough time and need some help. Sadness is to be expected, but if you become deeply depressed or hopeless, you need others (including a doctor) to help you get through this stage.

Talking about your grief can give you an outlet for your feelings. Sometimes it's especially helpful to talk to someone who is grieving with you so that you can laugh and cry together.

It also helps to distract yourself from grief, taking your mind off your sadness. Watch a movie or go to a party and don't be afraid to laugh. It's OK to have moments of joy when you are missing someone.

Honoring someone who has died is a great tribute. You can make a photo album or figure out your own way to remember that person in the future.

BEST GRANPA EVER ♡

GUILT

Feeling guilt with grief: Sometimes when we lose someone special, we feel guilty about the things we wish we had said to him or done with him. This feeling is very common. It's important to recognize that you can't go back in time, though. Allow yourself to feel the guilt, but then decide how you are going to change your life so that you don't have the same regrets with other people in the future. And if you're worried that you didn't tell a person how you truly felt about him, chances are you showed it. People know when they are loved.

If you just want to be left alone, try writing a letter about the person (or pet) you lost—you can keep it to yourself or share with others, but it helps to make a list of the things you value and you will miss.

WHAT I LOVED ABOUT YOU

Sometimes the loss isn't permanent. When a friend moves away, the loss can feel as big as any in your life. The same is true when you get in a big fight with someone and the two of you stop talking. These losses, though, aren't like death—they are fixable. Sure, there may be distance between you and your closest pal, but you can chat by phone, text, or video, and stay connected. You can also make plans to visit each other. If you've had a falling out with someone, you can work to repair the relationship. These fixes take effort, but they are worth the energy.

Eventually it helps to reconnect with other people in your community and share in their grief, too.

I FEEL....

I'M so EMBARRASSED

Embarrassment stretches anywhere from a small oops that makes you laugh all the way to deep humiliation. The type of embarrassment you'll feel depends partly on what happened and partly on who witnessed it.

The feeling: Embarrassment and blushing go hand in hand—your cheeks get red and feel warm, and you may even break out in a little sweat. When you're really embarrassed, though, the feeling can move into your chest and belly. Your heart might start to pound, or your stomach might feel queasy. The deepest form of embarrassment, called humiliation, can feel like anxiety or sadness. Another way people describe this feeling is shame.

The funny thing about being embarrassed is that it often has more to do with who sees, hears, or knows something than the actual thing itself. Think about being naked: There's nothing embarrassing about being naked alone in the shower. But if someone else sees you or even part of you without clothes on, that can feel embarrassing.

3 STRIKES!

YER OUT!

the GENERALS

I FEEL...

94

Humiliation and shame are feelings that run deep. The embarrassment here is so big that it can be hard to shake off the experience. It's important to talk to someone when you feel humiliated, because it's hard to get past this particular emotion on your own. You can try talking to the person who made you feel this way—that is, if it was one person and you feel the humiliation wasn't intentional. But often it's not a person, it's a whole situation. Find a good friend or trusted adult who can help you put things in perspective. No one is going to remember what happened as vividly as you will, and most likely, they won't remember at all.

Things that might make you feel a little (or a lot) embarrassed:

- If you try to make a couple of people laugh and your joke falls flat, you might feel a little self-conscious; but if you are standing on a stage trying to make a big group of people laugh and that falls flat, the humiliation is bigger.

- If a friend sees a text about you that's unflattering, you might feel a little awkward; but if that text gets passed around to a group of people you know and even people you don't know, you could feel embarrassed.

- If you strike out at bat during a practice game, you might feel a little cringey; but if you strike out in the ninth inning of the championship game, you might feel ashamed for losing it for the whole team.

I FEEL...

If you're just a little embarrassed, try laughing it off.

If you're feeling pretty awkward, take a deep breath and then carry on as if it didn't happen.

If you're feeling self-conscious and a little anxious, too, try setting the record straight with the people you care about.

If you are feeling embarrassed because you made a mistake that deserves an apology, give the apology. If you just made a mistake, forgive yourself.

If you are so embarrassed that you don't feel like you can show your face in public, you need help from an adult to get past this feeling. It's always OK to ask for help.

I FEEL....

97

I DON'T FEEL SAFE

There are definitely things in the world that make people feel unsafe. But there are also things that we worry about when we don't need to. How can you separate those two things? And how can you worry less by taking action?

The feeling: Feeling unsafe sits like a pit in the stomach. Sometimes it can cause belly pain, loss of appetite, headaches, or a racing heart. It can keep you up at night, especially if your imagination starts to run wild.

Worrying about bad things happening in the world is normal. The news, social media, and phone alerts almost always announce bad things, but there are rarely breaking stories about happy events. It's fair to get a little freaked out by the things you read or hear, especially when they are beyond your control.

Some people feel personally unsafe, thinking about the things that might happen to them; others worry about the safety of their friends, their family, or their community. There are people who feel unsafe and nervous about all these things, and there are people who don't worry about any of it. Your sense of safety will depend on your personality as much as it depends on the place where you live, the environment around you, and the resources you have.

You might feel unsafe if you have . . .

- been home alone and heard weird noises.

- been in an accident.

- read about school shootings or know someone who has been involved with gun violence.

- lived through a natural disaster, like a fire or an earthquake.

- been pressured to do something dangerous.

- been hurt by someone else, physically or emotionally.

If you worry about the safety of your home, talk to your parents about what you can do to make your environment more secure.

If you are freaked out by the news alerts that constantly announce negative events, turn off the TV and unplug from devices.

If you are stressed about being alone, come up with a system of communication with an adult so you can reach out if you need to.

I FEEL

If you are concerned that someone might hurt you, get help right away from an adult you trust.

Anytime you feel unsafe, the best choice is to talk to your parents. It's their job to keep you safe, so if you're not feeling that, they need to know. There are lots of other trusted adults that you can lean on, including older siblings and extended family members, teachers, coaches, and faith-community leaders. Friends your own age might not be the right choice when you need to talk about safety, because they cannot necessarily help you in the same way.

If your unsafe feeling is connected to the larger world—like climate change or human rights—find your voice and start to try to make change.

6 FEELING POSITIVE

Most of the time, you'll feel fine, good, or pretty darn great. When we talk about identifying and managing our feelings, these conversations tend to focus on being mad or sad, not glad. It's important to understand how to handle complex and negative emotions, but most of the time, your mood will likely be positive. And the positive and negative emotions definitely go together: The better you are at handling challenging emotions, the more you can resolve them and enjoy the good things in life.

THE GOOD STUFF

Just as there are lots of feelings that challenge us, we experience tons of different positive emotions, too. The list is pretty endless, but for starters . . .

RELAXED

appreciated

LOVED

trusted

RESPECTED

LIKED

GLAD

STOKED

inflated

IN CONTROL

SAFE

ZEN

Gratitude is the act of identifying what you are thankful for. Take a minute each day to focus on something positive and feel grateful. You can also say thank you to someone for what he's done to make you feel good. When someone tells you he appreciates what you did or said, it can fill you up in the best way. Pay that forward by telling someone else how much you value him.

THE WORLD is FULL of CHANGE

It's amazing to go through life experiencing all these different feelings. Positive ones and, yes, even negative ones, too.

Emotions play an enormous role in feeling vibrant and alive. They connect you with other people, particularly when you share similar feelings. And it's cool to think about the fact that everyone experiences the same wide range of feelings that you do—your parents, your teachers, and your friends all juggle these different types of emotions.

Knowledge is power. This is why it's so great to know how to identify your own feelings. If you can put words to what is happening inside your mind and your body, you will be able to share those emotions with other people much more easily. Even if you want to keep a feeling to yourself, there's great value in knowing how you feel and why you feel that way.

No one will ever know how you really feel unless you tell them. And you will never know how someone else feels unless you ask him. So ask him! Sharing this kind of information is what connects people. *Empathy* is the ability to feel for another person. It means putting yourself in his shoes and imagining life from his perspective. Developing empathy helps you connect more deeply to others around you. Ultimately, you will become more supportive in the things you say and the ways you act.

KEEP it UP!

When it comes to feelings, focus on your own emotional wellness first. Some people are so busy making sure everyone else is OK that they forget to take care of themselves. There's nothing wrong with taking time to understand how you feel about something. In fact, it's one of the keys to living a balanced life.

There isn't a person on earth who wouldn't rather be happy than sad. Now that you know how to identify and manage your own feelings better, start paying attention to how the people around you do the same thing. Learn from the ones who are able to deal with down times while also celebrating positives. All humans have feelings, regardless of their age, gender, or geography. Learning to deal with feelings in a healthy way is a big part of growing up, and continuing to use the tools in this book will help you become a strong and confident young man.

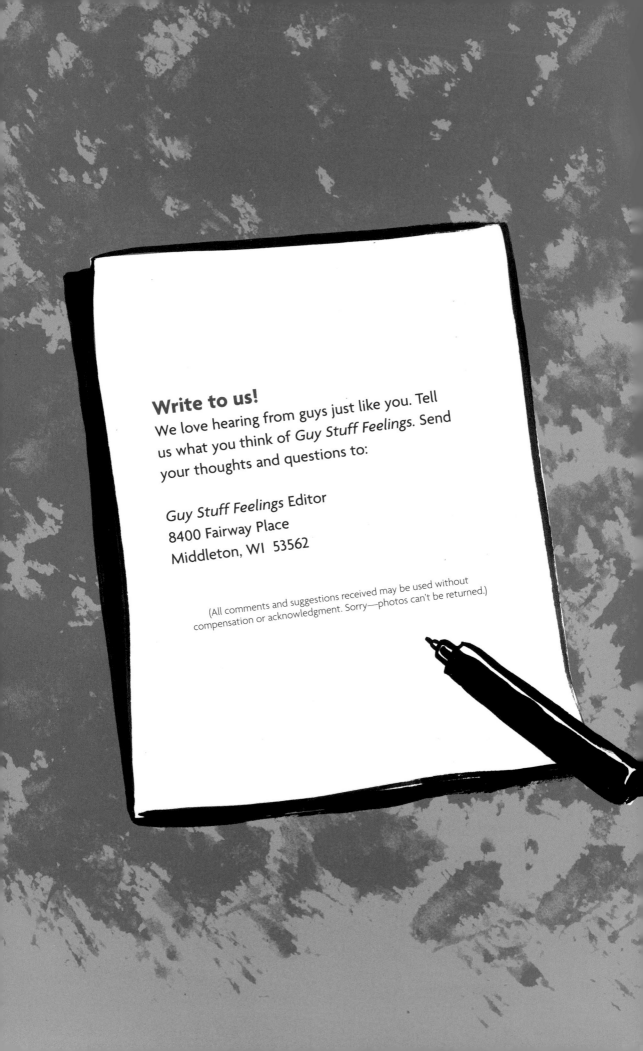

Write to us!

We love hearing from guys just like you. Tell us what you think of *Guy Stuff Feelings*. Send your thoughts and questions to:

Guy Stuff Feelings Editor
8400 Fairway Place
Middleton, WI 53562

(All comments and suggestions received may be used without compensation or acknowledgment. Sorry—photos can't be returned.)

You might also be interested in:

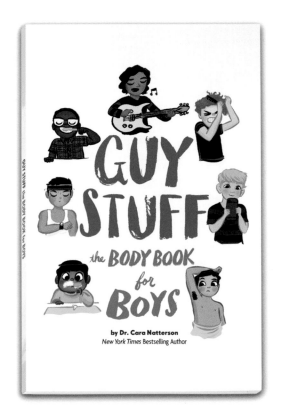

Sold separately.